THE BOOK OF THE
PATRIOT 4-6-0s

A Photographic Accompaniment:1

By Graham Onley

45551 with the odd looking Stanier high flat sided tender with which it ran from May 1958 to the end of its days. This came almost directly off 45515 and may have already had the 'wrong' right-side tender emblem at that time. It appears to have still been in situ (see parent book page 98) in June 1960, after which it was not likely ever to be changed. This photograph dates from 4 June 1959, and '55-51' appears to be dawdling through Preston on an up freight. Photograph A.W. Battson, www.transporttreasury.co.uk

IRWELL PRESS Ltd.

First published in the United Kingdom in 2007
by Irwell Press Limited, 59A, High Street, Clophill,
Bedfordshire MK45 4BE
Printed by Regal Litho, Milton Keynes

THE BOOK OF THE PATRIOT 4-6-0s
A Photographic Accompaniment: 1

When I first read through *The Book of the Patriot 4-6-0s* I thought, no doubt like most other readers, that I had probably been armed with just about all there was to say about the class in both mechanical terms and the operational reasons that brought them into being. When I was handed the opportunity, in the form of a large number of (largely) unused photographs, to enable us to prolong our gaze on their delicate (the originals) and their sturdily aggressive (the rebuilds) looks, I did not hesitate.

This 'Accompaniment' to the parent book purposely concentrates on what we saw from the lineside, particularly from Nationalisation up to the early 1960s. During this period matters slowly but surely improved after the dark days of wartime, which most of us still 'in stock' can barely imagine, until much of what we thought would last forever was swept away without ceremony.

As might be expected with a class which had 'North Western' parentage, most of their life and times was spent on the Western Division of the LMS and British Railways, London Midland Region, but I have attempted to show that both varieties of the Patriots did spend time on other lines or other Regions, even if in truth they only very rarely strayed, in service, away from what can clearly be seen as ex-LMS lines and sheds.

After the twelve post-Harrow Princess Royal Pacifics, the thirty-four original Patriots were the next smallest in number of LMS passenger classes. Generally speaking, this was evident from the lineside, where, by day at least, the ninety-one class 7P 4-6-0s were far and away the staple diet of enthusiasts ranging the length of the west coast lines. It was here that they were almost exclusively allocated, and from where, despite my own partial failure, hindsight reminds me that even the Holbeck and Polmadie Royal Scots could eventually be gathered up with patience!

The fact that the parallel boilered Patriots were relatively scarce, and positively old-fashioned to our young eyes, turned us misty eyed when one was about. For a short period starting in the latest months of the 1950s Rugby, and later Nuneaton, received a small allocation of the Baby Scots, and I found them in our local area to a greater extent. They were very welcome too, especially when they turned up increasingly more often 'on the shed' at Northampton, making us feel more privileged than in earlier days when a Stanier Class 5 would normally have been the best on offer. 45533, 45537, 45538, 45541, 45542 and 45548 were the engines involved, and having inspected the parent 'Book Of', I now realise why 45542 seems a bit scarce in my memory – it came from the somewhat distant Preston to Nuneaton late in July 1961 and within three months went into the short, dead end siding of storage and scrapping.

The commencement of withdrawal of the non-rebuilt engines was hardly a surprise, and the day of the Baby Scots at our end of the western division was effectively over well before the end of 1961, and generally by the late summer of 1962. Luckily

As Longsight-allocated 45500 was transferred to Carlisle Upperby in November 1954, and *The Railway Observer* noted PATRIOT to be in BR dark green livery by March 1952, when fresh from general repair, the period of this picture has to fall between those two dates. The lighting indicates Crewe North as the likely spot.

the rebuilds were still as visible as ever even if, from 1961 onwards they fell, somewhat later, into the same pattern of the parallel boilered engines, reduced to 'the better class of freight'. There was only the occasional, declining, opportunity to show their express paces.

As is well known, the rebuilds lasted until late 1965, but the removal of 45514 from the scene in May 1961 was the shock which confirmed our growing fears that the downward spiral of change on the railway side of our lives was likely to accelerate. How right we were!

Like the other LMS passenger classes, the advent of nationalisation led to coats of many colours, with numerous examples of alterations only to insignia and numberplates, creating what I can only describe as 'sub liveries'. It was only during late hours spent poring over the marvellous collection of photographs bequeathed to us by well known photographers from far and wide, and gathered together by the 'brass' at Irwell Press that I realised that, despite having previously seen pictures of locomotives both in BR mixed traffic black with BRITISH RAILWAYS in full on the tender, and the same basic livery with the first BR tender emblem, I had not actually registered the fact. I am not sure that this particular livery route was taken by a Patriot, but Jubilee 45700 is one that did – but that is one for the future! I own up to being fascinated by early BR colour schemes, most probably due to having been around in those times but was too young to notice much other than numbers and names as trains passed. The rarely removed grime rapidly alighting on any colour scheme of the time was little incentive for the average spotter of under ten years old to notice either the fascinating liveries or the minor variations within. Yet again I give thanks and acknowledgement to the 'RO' and those stalwarts who noted such minutiae, as well as the photographers whose work appears in this 'Accompaniment'. I recently acquired an all-singing and all-dancing digital camera – how many of us have wondered what we might have produced had we arrived ten years earlier and the digital camera fifty years earlier!

This photograph of 45500, still a Longsight engine (as it was until November 1954) gives us another look at the huge 'Claughton' type wheel centres and the fluted coupling rods, unique to 45500 and 45501 amongst the Patriots, and which they both retained until their ultimate end. Photograph www.transporttreasury.co.uk

Towards the end of its working life, 45500 was, in effect, promoted (from Carnforth) to the heady heights of Newton Heath (26A). This is 45500 bringing empty coaches into Manchester Victoria on 3 September 1960; PATRIOT's future stretched only as far as March of the following year. Underneath the grime it may be assumed that the second tender emblem lurks pointlessly. Photograph B.W.L. Brooksbank, Initial Photographics.

45501 ST. DUNSTAN'S standing shabbily and quietly at Shrewsbury shed. It is safe to say that was not running in after a general overhaul! The engine got AWS in February 1959 and has not yet been fitted with electrification flashes – the period, we can fairly safely say, is 1959-mid-1960. The AWS timer, a small cylinder, can be seen ahead of the cab on the running plate.

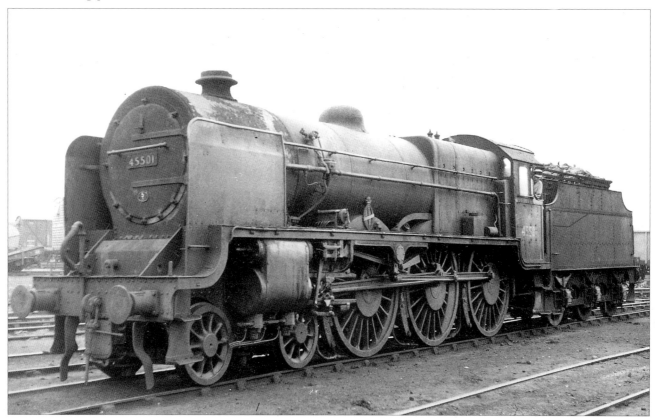

There is a strong North Western atmosphere to this portrait amongst the trees at what appears to be Carnforth shed. 45502 was to be the first Patriot withdrawal, during August 1960. The 12A shedplate indicates a date prior to Upperby's 'demotion' to 12B in February 1958. The foliage and the immaculate condition of ROYAL NAVAL DIVISION could indicate that the photograph was taken soon after the engine's release from its last general repair, completed by 2 October 1957. Photograph Eric Blakey, www.transporttreasury.co.uk

45503 had became a 'Royal' Regiment by 1948 and was renamed accordingly. This led to it getting one of the very few 'stepped' nameplates amongst former LMS engines, which can be seen clearly here. THE ROYAL LEICESTERSHIRE REGIMENT is at home on Crewe North shed on 9 May 1954. Considering that 45503 received a heavy intermediate repair during June/July 1953, and was about to be called back within days of this photograph, it would seem that the 1950s may not always have been the filthy wasteland we sometimes choose to remember and that Crewe North was quite able to put on a show when it felt like it. Photograph B.K.B. Green, Initial Photographics.

Grime had, however, well and truly overtaken 45503 by the time it was seen heading north through Preston with a fitted freight on 19 June 1961. Photograph A.W. Battson, www.transporttreasury.co.uk

Above. The occasion of the annual Crewe works Open Day on 9 August 1961 found 45503 apparently awaiting attention; note the engine number stencilled over removable parts. It was not to be however, for the engine was withdrawn and reduced to scrap during September 1961. In the same distress, behind super-D 49430, lies Newton Heaths' 45509, which was also still bearing nameplates and front numberplate. Photograph Graham Onley.

Below. The November 1958 transfer of three original Patriots, 45504, 45506 and 45519, to the Western Region, albeit to a 'proper' Midland/LMS shed at Bristol Barrow Road, was a little surprising, and was truly resented at Duston West, Northampton's very own heart of trainspotting on Earth. It was felt that they would disappear from our orbit, other than the aftermath of visits to Crewe works which might see them temporarily set loose on the Western Division. It was confidently expected that the WR would send them back home, but the three doggedly held on until they were all despatched to Crewe for scrap during February 1962. Here 45504 ROYAL SIGNALS, complete with 82E shedplate, and destined never to receive AWS gear, looks distinctly unloved as it restarts the 2.15pm Bristol-York express through Bromsgrove station, after banking aid has buffered up, on 18 August 1960. Photograph B.W.L. Brooksbank, Initial Photographics.

Above. 45506 THE ROYAL PIONEER CORPS of Crewe North in Crewe works yard on 5 February 1950, awaiting a heavy intermediate repair. The locomotive is reasonably respectable in the commendable British Railways mixed traffic black livery it received late in 1948, still awaiting the (never received) addition of a BR emblem between the words on the tender. The cabside also carries the 5XP branding above the numbers. This particular repair was, according to the parent book, completed within twenty three working days, so it is probable that BR green had to await the general repair received in the autumn of 1951. The crosshead still has the four bolt mounting plate for the arm which once operated the vacuum pump, bolted to the lower slidebar. Photograph R.J. Buckley, Initial Photographics.

Below. In weak light, the last vestiges of an early 1962 snowfall survive on the grass alongside the signalbox as 45505 THE ROYAL ARMY ORDNANCE CORPS enters Keighley with a Bradford-Morecambe train. Lancaster shed (24J) acquired (or was saddled with) a number of original members of the class from February 1962 for trains such as this, and from May of the same year this most unlikely of sheds boasted (well perhaps not boasted) all of the last six survivors, four of which soon went into store prior to withdrawal, leaving two (45543 and 45550) to be transferred to Carnforth, where they may or may not have been happily received. The two then saw out the days of the original version, and despite surviving fully intact in the burnt out remains of Preston shed until at least 20 July 1963, were cut up at Crewe during the September. Had they remained hidden a while longer, one of them may have managed to make it into preservation. I believe that at least the last of the Claughtons, George the Fifths and Precursors were accorded a family snapshot at Crewe before they were dispatched after a tantalising period had elapsed. Photograph Brian Lister.

On 6 August 1955 45506 THE ROYAL PIONEER CORPS of Carlisle Upperby finds gentle relaxation at the head of a six coach southbound express passing what looks to be the run in towards the start of Hest Bank water troughs. Photograph R. Butterfield, Initial Photographics.

45506 THE ROYAL PIONEER CORPS carries the unfamiliar 82E shedplate, as well as scorching on the smokebox door, as its rests at home on Bristol Barrow Road shed. The period would be late 1959-early 1960. Native Western Region 2-6-0 6376 sits behind, probably feeling more of a foreigner that the Patriot. Photograph R.C. Riley, www.transporttreasury.co.uk

Birmingham New Street was always a cross roads of the whole system, and here is one of the many trains that plied the north-east to south-west axis. On 30 July 1960 the 12.52pm York-Bristol express enters platform 9 past No.2 box under the eye of a spotter who looks a little better dressed than the norm of the times. He must have come from other than the London Midland Region if 45506 (82E) was a new number for him – or perhaps it was his first visit to New Street! Within a matter of weeks the first Patriot withdrawals were upon us. The flood of Type 4s was to quickly wash away all the Barrow Road Patriots (for scrap) and Jubilees (to Shrewsbury) with the exception of 45682 and 45690 which clung on at Barrow Road into 1964. Photograph Michael Mensing.

A broadside 45507 ROYAL TANK CORPS at its home shed Crewe North shed on 9 May 1954. The 'Book of' indicates that 45507 was in the course of a twenty-six day heavy intermediate repair at that time, but I would be happy to take the photographer's word and accept that the works staff were happy to carry out what is now called 'creative accounting' to keep the bean counters, and hence the boss, happy. How attractive these locomotives looked from any angle, especially this one. Photograph B.K.B. Green, Initial Photographics.

Upperby's 45508 looking contented enough in Crewe works yard on 9 August 1953, after a light repair. A little over three years passed before 45508 suffered the indignity of the dreadful stove pipe chimney with which it was to end its days. Although it was one of the few Baby Scots that I was happy not to set eyes upon after the end of 1956. Although it was already in my Ian Allan ABC, it was one of the few Baby Scots that I was happy not to set eyes upon after the end of 1956. Although it would probably not have occurred to the spotters of the time, those responsible must have known that it was getting a little late in the day for meaningful experiments! Photograph B.K.B. Green, Initial Photographics.

12

After the removal of the last original Patriots (45534, 45535 and 45538) from Leeds Holbeck in 1948 and until the arrival of 45504, 45506 and 45519 at Bristol Barrow Road in late 1958, 45509 was the only Patriot to be allocated to a former Midland Railway shed. It had arrived from Crewe North in October 1951 on loan, being recorded as a permanent transfer from the day of its naming as THE DERBYSHIRE YEOMANRY on 10 November 1951. It is difficult not to see the naming and the transfer as part of one idea, which may or may not have been a good one in operational terms. Here it is looking the part, heading south-west out of Derby with the 12.45pm Newcastle-Bristol express on 16 May 1952. Photograph R.J. Buckley, Initial Photographics.

The novelty of having a locally named Patriot on the allocation may have worn a little thin judging by the lack of cleaning, by 28 February 1954. Note also the smokebox char left on the front bufferbeam – I imagine this would eventually have removed itself once 45509 got under way! Whatever was behind its transfer to Derby, it made life a little more difficult at Duston West in particular and the Western Division in general! Photograph B.K.B. Green, Initial Photographics.

It was probably only a light snow shower, but it certainly made for what appears to be a raw cold day as 45510 heaved a long fitted freight south through Tamworth on 8 March 1958. Until the arrival of the D200 diesels sent a good number of the class to new homes further north, and ultimately to the scrapheap, 45510, being based mainly at Willesden or Crewe North in the 1950s was one of those locomotives that we just KNEW was going to turn up, and it frequently did! Photograph Michael Mensing.

45511 ISLE OF MAN was to suffer the same fate as 45510, being sent from Willesden to Carnforth in October 1959. In far more settled days, 45511 is doing what she did most of the time (being a Willesden engine) that is, heading a northbound fitted freight past a familiar sight at Lichfield in 1955. This would probably have bounced and swayed merrily past our site at Blisworth a couple of hours or so previously. I wonder how many of the spotters in this picture knew that there was a Cold War in progress – even if times were perhaps not that settled, they didn't look too concerned! Photograph www.transporttreasury.co.uk

To remember 5512 in its parallel boiler days you need to be somewhere in the region of at least 65 years of age. For those of us who cannot go back quite that far, here is an eventual rebuild in the condition that a previous generation have often said they preferred. I personally think that having both types was the best available option. When BUNSEN was photographed wearing the 1B shedplate of Camden on Crewe South shed on 10 October 1937, was it possible that the germ of what led to the rebuilding of the two Jubilees, and ultimately the Royal Scots and eighteen Patriots was already in Stanier's mind when he decided to make some use of the redundant chassis of the high pressure 4-6-0 6399 FURY in creating 6170 BRITISH LEGION?

Preston station provided rich pickings for many a photographer. 45512 BUNSEN, after a first winter as a rebuild, (based at Bushbury) went to Carlisle Upperby, only moving for its last few months down the road to Kingmoor. Here is the old burner (alas, how could we resist?) passing Preston on 11 June 1963 in a rather disreputable condition, at the head of a down fitted freight. The non-standard looking stock to the immediate left of the platform side smoke deflector appears to be a National Coal Board travelling exhibition extolling the virtues of coal-fired central heating. What goes round may yet come round... Photograph A.W. Battson, www.transporttreasury.co.uk

I believe that BUNSEN had from time to time been well groomed by Upperby for use on football specials at a time when Carlisle United F.C. was on a good run in the Football League and/or the F.A. Cup. Here he is recreating old times and still wearing nameplates, heading a down express bound for Scotland past Preston under a fixed distant on 26 March 1964, and looking every inch the part. By then Carlisle were heading from the old Fourth Division to a single season in the First Division in 1974-75. I would just add that Northampton Town made the same journey, with the same end (relegation) by 1965-66. Photograph A.W. Battson, www.transporttreasury.co.uk

A little late in the Patriot story, even if not quite a minute to midnight! The un-named 45513 of Carnforth is entrusted with an Anglo-Scottish express of a size not usually associated with the last years of the original members of the class. The twelve coach 1S47 is near Crawford on 5 August 1961. Even allowing that this was a summer Saturday, it would surely have been reasonable to expect that sufficient D200 type diesels and 7P/8P steam locomotives would have been available, so this may be an instance of the rostered locomotive having failed en route. Photograph A.W. Battson, J.L. Stevenson, courtesy Hamish Stevenson.

Nine days after release from Crewe works after a heavy general, 45514 HOLYHEAD of Camden is moving a Crewe-bound local out of Manchester London Road, on 1 April 1957. The overhaul had included a repaint and one of the earliest 'production' applications of the second tender emblem, which at that early date, quite incorrectly, sported forward facing lions on each side of the tender. It is well enough known now that this did not meet the requirements of the College of Heralds; their diktat was that the lion had to face only to the left, which meant that the emblem on the right side (looking forward) had to face the rear of the tender. Photograph B.K.B. Green, Initial Photographics.

By 31 May 1959 HOLYHEAD was not quite as pristine as it headed an up express past South Kenton. A glass confirms that the 'wrong' tender emblem is still in situ. On this particular Sunday, main line traffic was again diverted our way, and, sure enough 45514 (1B) appears on my three session-long Duston West listing as passing with a down express just after the late evening passage of the down 'Royal Highlander' (behind 71000) so it would appear that, even for a Sunday, 45514 was doing its bit and more. It was not to continue – soon after the turn of the year enough English Electric Type 4 diesels had become available for 45514 to be moved on to the Midland division at Millhouses. The 'paper' transfer from what was then an Eastern Region shed to Derby (17A) in May 1961 can be ignored; the significance was that it led to, or was led by, the first withdrawal of a rebuilt Patriot. Scrapping was at Crewe works during June 1961, and it poses the question as to whether 45514 actually bypassed Derby and headed direct to Crewe Photograph Alec Swain, www.transporttreasury.co.uk

By far the bulk of its BR life was spent working from Edge Hill from where 45515 CAERNARVON would have ranged far and wide over the west coast and the cross-Pennine routes. Here it is clambering up Camden bank with a motley collection of coaches purporting to represent a Euston to Liverpool Lime Street express. The quoted date of 21 August 1955 was a Sunday, and I wonder if in fact we might be looking at an Edge Hill engine filling in its weekend in London with an outer suburban train. Photograph R.C. Riley, www.transporttreasury.co.uk

A Bournemouth-bound Saturday holiday extra is about to depart from Lime Street on 13 June 1959 behind home-based 45515. The crew have moved their attention from the 'right away' end to the photographer. Between the dates of this and the preceding photograph, 45515 had a brief eight months flirtation with Stanier high flat sided tenders 4573 and 4570. See page 50 of the parent 'Book Of'. Photograph B.W.L. Brooksbank, Initial Photographics.

On 17 February 1950 the Southern Region Public Relations and Publicity Department photographer was on hand at Southampton where the eponymous 45516 of far-away Preston was making ready to collect a special boat train conveying soldiers of the 1ˢᵗ Battalion of the Bedfordshire and Hertfordshire Regiment to a place 'somewhere in England' (actually within the confines of the western division of the London Midland Region). Not only would the Preston shedplate and the LMS legend on the tender excite the locals, but it might very well have been their first sight in steam of surviving LMS maroon livery, even if with a BR number, on home soil. By 15 June 1950 45516 was to disappear into Crewe works, where the less exotic BR mixed traffic black livery would replace the maroon. In times then far away into the future (or so it seemed) ex-LMS express engines up to rebuilt Royal Scots would occasionally tread this path pioneered by 45516.

45516 on 23 September 1951 (a date I wouldn't challenge) during the period (19 September 1951 to 5 July 1952) when it was allocated to Carlisle Upperby (12A). It is at Cheadle Hulme with the 4.05pm Manchester-London express, running with tender 3187, as it had since February 1935 with the first BR emblem. Photograph T. Lewis, Norman Preedy Collection.

Here is a less contentious shot of 45516, halted on the up through road in Stafford station early on the morning of Good Friday 31 March 1961 with a partially fitted freight. Withdrawal beckoned by the end of July of the same year. The DMU at the down platform had recently arrived as the 6.23am from Coventry. Photograph Michael Mensing.

I can personally vouch for the fact that 45517 was, shall we say, a rather frequent performer on western division metals during the mid-1950s. It was one of eleven working at various times, frequently on 'the better sort of freight' (see page 40 of the parent book) from Willesden shed, rivalled only by 45510, 45511 and 45546 for longevity. Before its transfer to Bank Hall and minor celebrity, the ever-nameless 45517 is near to London with a partially fitted freight; the view is from the footbridge just to the north of Hatch End station and the train is on the up fast, unusually for what appears to be an unfitted freight (that mineral wagon next to the engine is unlikely to be vacuum braked). The Bushey troughs are beyond the overbridge in the background; to the left are the DC lines.

Having acquired its only Patriot, Bank Hall did not seem to expend much – if any, by the look of it here – manpower in keeping it clean. 45517 is standing in a quiet if rather messy corner of the extensive and strung out complex that was York shed on 30 August 1959, between jobs on the cross Pennine road. AWS gear had been fitted a couple of months or so previously. Photograph Alec Swain, www.transporttreasury.co.uk

I know this is a forlorn picture, but it was par for the original Patriot course from 1961 onwards. 45517 stands, apparently empty of coal, at Bank Hall shed on 10 May 1962, having gone into store from early the previous month. Withdrawal came early in June and scrapping was completed during July 1962. The original Patriot story was as good as over. Photograph A.W. Battson, www.transporttreasury.co.uk

Photographers were out in force on Saturday 29 July 1961 when 45517 headed the 9.30am Southport to Glasgow Saturday relief express past, firstly, Beattock and secondly, Symington. Although 45517 was acknowledged as a regular visitor to Scotland in its Bank Hall days, by 1961 *any* original Patriot would have been a surprising visitor north of the border. Photographs W.A.C. Smith; J.L. Stevenson, courtesy Hamish Stevenson.

BRADSHAW appears to be in light steam 'round the back' at what is surely Polmadie. The livery is, for the dismal times, a reasonably tidy LMS 1946 Black, with the maroon footplating and the straw lining making a brave effort. 45518 was renumbered as such early in July 1948. It is possible that the LMS part of the black livery gave way to BR mixed traffic black during BRADSHAW's forty-four days of general overhaul which started from 19 December 1950, since the 'Railway Observer' tells us that 45518 was one of the few express engines still in some form of black livery as far on as about March 1954. This being so, and in conjunction with the 12B (Carlisle Upperby) shedplate, the date will be sometime between July 1948 and December 1950. The smokebox numberplate would eventually be replaced by the standard version. Photograph J. Robertson, www.transporttreasury.co.uk

The 9th of January 1960 was a Saturday, so despite the mid-winter period, there would have been a few spotters about. 45518, almost at the end of its more than six years at Edge Hill, arrives at Rugeley (Trent Valley) with the 11.45 semi-fast from Liverpool Lime Street to Rugby Midland. There is nearly a full house in the offing – pity that just above the second coach of the train the up main line signal can be seen to be 'on'. Photograph Michael Mensing.

By my reckoning 45518 BRADSHAW was one of the last six original Patriots to be 'officially' active; by the date of this photograph, 25 April 1962, it had 45505, 45507 and 45510 sharing its roost at Lancaster (Green Ayre). Eventually all four could stave off storage and withdrawal no longer. The number even increased to six for the blink of an eye when 45543 and 45550 joined them from Edge Hill and Warrington respectively on 5 May. By 2 June 45543 and 45550 had been sent on to Carnforth, where they were to become the last of the class 'on the books'. In this picture, 45518 is about to leave Wennington Junction with the Leeds and Bradford to Morecambe portion of a train with a further portion also for Carnforth. Photograph F.W. Shuttleworth.

This undated photograph shows 45519 LADY GODIVA, now of Bristol Barrow Road, receiving banking assistance from an unidentified engine as she climbs the Lickey incline with the northbound 'Devonian'. The parent book tells us that prior to transfer from Carlisle Upperby in September 1958, 45519 had a general repair completed during the July. The reasonably clean condition, with second tender emblem and the obvious winter conditions lead me to plump for an approximate date of January/February 1959, since for most of the following winter of 1959/60 she was in Crewe works. I could be wrong, but '55-19' was not at all clean when photographed in September 1959. See below. Photograph Stanley Creer, www.transporttreasury.co.uk

45519 LADY GODIVA looks to be coasting as she passes Castle Bromwich station with the up 'Devonian' on 5 September 1959. Photograph Michael Mensing.

Longsight was hardly a hot-bed of original Patriots during the 1950s in the way that, say, Crewe North was. Any reader caring to carry out a rough check from the parent book will find that only six (45500, 45501, 45515, 45519, 45520 and 45537) actually managed to put a reasonable amount of time in! Of these 45520 LLANDUDNO was far and away the longest serving – unbroken from June 1948 to December 1960 except for the currency of the 1956 summer timetable, which saw it exiled to Preston. My own perception of 45520 on the occasions our paths crossed was that it always seemed to be in the immaculate condition normally associated on the western division only with ex-works engines. Here are two shots of it which prove my point, leaving Manchester London Road on 26 February and passing Cheadle Hulme on 22 March 1953. Both trains are described as Manchester-Birmingham expresses, although the Cheadle Hulme shot has a doubtful show of lamps and stock. Photographs B.K.B. Green, Initial Photographics.

The rebuilt 45521 RHYL was an early recipient of BR dark green livery and smoke deflectors (by about March 1950) although it retained its original Stanier top feed. This undated picture shows it after arrival at Euston with the 'Merseyside Express', not long after rebuilding judging by the composition of the train, there being no sign of any BR Mark 1 stock. An Edge Hill engine from June 1947 until September 1961 (when it probably didn't matter anyway) it may have been a planned replacement for the more normal Princess Royal Pacific. Photograph Paul Chancellor Collection.

Showing signs of neglect, but still allocated to Edge Hill and rostered for top link work, 45521 RHYL would have been on one of its last few such jobs when it was photographed waiting to take over a southbound express at Carlisle Citadel on 12 August 1961. The oblivion that was Springs Branch was beckoning. Photograph Norman Preedy.

On 20 April 1957 rebuilt 45521 RHYL is looking reasonably tidy as it passes Crewe station with the 2.10pm Liverpool Lime Street to Euston express. The Ivatt style top feed has arrived. The annual mileages of 45521 (and no doubt many others) generally held up through to the end of 1960, and then slumped dramatically as modernisation advanced, leading in this case to transfer to Springs Branch (8F *nee* 10A) and what would seem a reasonably dignified downhill run to retirement. Photograph A.W. Battson, www.transporttreasury.co.uk

The newly rebuilt 45522 PRESTATYN, the last of the eighteen Patriots to be so treated, looking magnificent at Crewe works on 6 February 1949. It did of course receive the Ivatt top feed from the start, and like the previous seven rebuilds went straight into what eventually became the pure BR mixed traffic black livery, still with a 6P power classification under the cabside number. On entering the works as the unrebuilt 5522 allocated to Preston, it left as 45522 and was to be allocated to Crewe North. This probably explains the lack of a shedplate. The picture also indicates that it had not been long before the well known non-serif style of smokebox numberplate came into use.

45522 had arrived on Camden's allocation in mid 1950, and despite transfer away with the advent of the diesels, still managed to stay in London, moving (sort of) round the north circular road to Kentish Town. In this photograph, taken at Holyhead shed on 29 March 1959, a few months before D210 and its fellows began to assert themselves, PRESTATYN is now looking less reputable. The 'wrong' tender emblem can just be made out under the gathering grime. Photograph J.L. Stevenson, courtesy Hamish Stevenson.

Above. By the time a presumably grateful and appreciative Kentish Town got hold of 45522 late in 1959, it had been through Crewe works, where it seems to have been necessary to have more than one bite at the cherry. This attention had brought along AWS gear and a speedometer, despite allocation to a line where AWS would not have been required! Here PRESTATYN simmers at Kentish Town soon after transfer. 45522 was to find itself back on home territory at Longsight from June 1963 until withdrawal in September 1964, when, alone amongst the Patriots, the yellow cab side stripe was painted on inside the cab lining, rather than corner to corner. Photograph J. Davenport, Initial Photographics.

Left. Camden's immaculate rebuild 45523 BANGOR at Crewe North on 28 March 1954. The parent 'Book Of' confirms that a general overhaul, which would have included a BR green repaint, was completed on or about 25 March. The equally immaculate locomotive almost buffered up to 45523 has a previously un-noticed (well, by me anyway!) detail difference, and is obviously a rebuilt Royal Scot. I was aware that the front end view of the Patriot bufferbeams differed from that of the Scots, but I had never noticed that from side-on the footplating vertical on both the original and the rebuilt Scots was turned downwards, but was not so on both types of Patriot. Oh well... Photograph A.W. Battson, www.transporttreasury.co.uk

Above. It is documented that at various dates after dieselisation had taken a hold over matters, Willesden shed received a number of 7P rebuilds of all three types. One of the Patriots was 45523 BANGOR, which I can well testify had long been a Camden engine! On 21 December 1962 BANGOR was at Willesden, only days after emerging from storage at Devons Road. 45523 would continue working through until further storage started on 2 October 1963 followed only by withdrawal. Although the nameplates had been refitted in December 1962, the right-hand one at least had disappeared by May 1963. Photograph Hamish Stevenson.

Top right. The shedplate carried by a thoroughly unkempt 45524 BLACKPOOL seems to show a single digit number, which I take to indicate probably 8B Warrington or possibly 8A Edge Hill. The location is assuredly Birkenhead shed and the period between September 1960 and June 1961, noting that 47005 and what is surely 47164 were both allocated there together when, moreover, AWS and electrification flashes were part of 45524. Photograph Paul Chancellor Collection.

Right. Not only is rebuilt Patriot 45525 COLWYN BAY, a long-time resident of Edge Hill pictured at Holyhead shed on 8 September 1957, now part of history but so are the useful cycle clips. No doubt in the fullness of time the purposeful, as against dangling, 'fag' of the shed man will likewise pass into the realm of folklore. On a slightly more serious note, I wonder if Edge Hill engines often reached Anglesey, or is this another piece of ex-works running in after the heavy intermediate repair then only recently completed on 45525. Photograph Frank Hornby.

45526 MORECAMBE and HEYSHAM had arrived at its final shed Carlisle Upperby as far back as June 1950, wearing that shed's changing plates 12A and 12B over the years between then and withdrawal in October 1964. Manoeuvring within the boundaries of Upperby on 13 June 1964, it is noteworthy for still retaining its nameplates; the benighted (or is it benighting?) cab-side stripe denoting its impending removal from the action south of Crewe is yet to appear. The top lamp bracket is still in its rightful place. Photograph J.L. Stevenson, courtesy Hamish Stevenson.

Despite O.S. Nock's well-argued dislike of the naming policy, if such there was, for the Patriots, I do not recollect hearing anyone voice displeasure at the variety to be found. The fact that there were some engines without names, and the possibility that they might be named at some time in the future seemed only to add to the fun. Perhaps I had a natural bias, but I enjoyed them all, and considered the style of the plates neat, tidy and unfussy, whether painted black or red. The nameplate with coat of arms atop generally meant the assembly 'sat' directly on the splasher, although a small number, such as on 45525, proves this to be not quite universal.
Photograph A.W. Battson,
www.transporttreasury.co.uk

45526 MORECAMBE and HEYSHAM had obviously been engaged in some hard graft even before it was photographed making an unaided climb of Shap with a lengthy fitted freight in August 1964. Nameplates still look to be in situ, the cab side stripe has been added ready for September 1, and the top and middle buffer beam lamp bracket have been re-sited since 13 June. Photograph J.G. Walmsley, www.transporttreasury.co.uk

SOUTHPORT effectively spent its working life (original and rebuilt) at Edge Hill, with a further almost irrelevant six sheds and eight transfers following during the last three and a half years leading to withdrawal in December 1964. The front facing cab window shows possible signs of a recent works visit. This picture was taken at some time during its spell at Holyhead shed after May 1961.

A rear end view of 45527 SOUTHPORT, probably taken at Carlisle Upperby soon after the yellow cab side stripe was added in about July or August 1964. For the time, SOUTHPORT looks reasonably presentable; the cabside has been properly cleaned to ensure that the yellow stripe 'took'. It was unlikely to retain its nameplates for much longer though. Perhaps O.S. Nock would have approved! SOUTHPORT effectively spent its working life (original and rebuilt) at Edge Hill, with a further almost irrelevant six sheds and eight transfers following during the last three and a half years up to withdrawal in December 1964.

45528 of Crewe North looks very respectable with a Manchester London Road to London Euston express near Cheadle Hulme. The date is not given, but the overall carriage livery of carmine and cream with not a Mark 1 in sight leads me to estimate the early 1950s. This is supported by the presence of the first tender emblem (45528 might just have been amongst the first to qualify for the second emblem on finishing a general repair in March 1957) and also by the front footplate grab rail still being on the footplating rather than near the base of the smoke deflector as had become the norm from sometime in the early-mid part of the decade. Photograph B.K.B. Green, Initial Photographics.

This undated picture at Camden shed is unusual in that two rebuilt Patriots are on view. Behind 45528 is 45521, ready to drop down to Euston for the 'Manxman'. 45528 had become R.E.M.E. in October 1959; this, the level of grime after a (presumably spruced up) naming and the absence of electrification warning flashes (although the Black 5 behind 45528 with the look of a recent works visit is so attired) indicate an odds-on late spring/early summer 1960 date. AWS gear had arrived early in 1960 and the speedometer would appear during the summer of 1961. Note also the smoke deflector handrail on both 7Ps.

The mightiest oak must topple in the end; R.E.M.E., in store, nameplates already removed at Willesden roundhouse on 21 December 1962, was withdrawn by the following January. 45528 would end its life having not seen active service since the end of the 1962 summer timetable. Photograph J.L. Stevenson, courtesy Hamish Stevenson.

I was surprised as a seven year old (give or take a year) to discover that there was, amongst the rebuilt Patriots, one without a name, 45528. The Duston West squad, in those days before the arrival of the 9F 2-10-0s, contended that anything with smoke deflectors should have been a 'namer'. I eventually discovered that 45529 had been another, only becoming STEPHENSON in the summer of 1948. On 21 August 1955 45529, which between May 1949 and April 1958 moved from Crewe North to Camden and vice versa on eight separate occasions, was photographed in traditional pose on Camden shed already coaled and facing northwards. Another instance of the front footplating handrail still to move upwards to the base of the smoke deflector. Photograph R.C. Riley, www.transporttreasury.co.uk

Four young lads (look above the tender) cannot help but stop whatever they were doing to watch as 45530 SIR FRANK REE heads a fitted freight through Preston northbound (at a risky guess). The external condition of 45530 would indicate that the photograph was taken during the summer of 1963 whilst it was in the care of Willesden shed.

By 29 May 1965 at St Rollox a down at heel 45530 had lost its respectable paintwork and its name but had gained the unfortunate yellow cab side stripe. 45530 still looked business-like, especially at the front end, where I consider the smoke deflectors, useless or otherwise, to have made the 7Ps look purposeful when compared to their earlier appearance without them.

I have included this photograph of 45531 SIR FREDERICK HARRISON in order to offer thanks for the decision to dispense with the light green livery inflicted upon it and a few of the (then) 5XP and 6P classes. Here he is working from Bushbury shed, leaving Birmingham New Street with a Wolverhampton to Euston express on 23 July 1948. 45531 endured the livery until at least September 1950, but was noted in the much more acceptable BR green by August 1951. The end of its general overhaul in June/July 1951 would have been the time of repainting. The leading coach appears to be part of the train that was painted in plum and spilt milk experimental coach livery. Photograph B.W.L. Brooksbank, Initial Photographics.

Above. 45531 SIR FREDERICK HARRISON seemed to be a regular at any Western Division location at which I found myself! Here, rather late in the day, despite modernisation, it was still shedded at Edge Hill and was still able to find Sunday employment. On 2 September 1962, unusually for the period carrying a smokebox headboard, 45531 opens up for the five miles at 1 in 200 to rejoin the main line at Roade Junction after the mandatory 20 mph speed restriction through Northampton Castle station. The train is the up 'Ulster Express'. Photograph Graham Onley.

Below. Nottingham shed was a beneficiary of the perceived turn round in fortune which gave the western division a surplus of 7P (and eventually 8P power) from the autumn of 1959. The powers that be had decided that the English Electric Type 4 diesels had got their feet under the table, despite the fact that they never really did! Part of this benefit included the November 1959 transfer of 45532 ILLUSTRIOUS from Camden. It looks as if the bloke who fitted the 16A shedplate might have had a tin of red paint with him and did the deed with the nameplate, which added a welcome extra splash of colour. 45532 is about to depart St. Pancras with the 12.55pm to Leicester on 26 February 1960. Photograph L.J. Farmer.

It is doubtful that Upperby's 45533 LORD RATHMORE would make many more visits to Polmadie after this one on 17 July 1959. By November of that year he had been transferred south to Rugby and later to Nuneaton, before moving back to the old stamping ground of Edge Hill in September 1961. There, he was 'available for traffic' for a mere two months, before a lengthy period of storage followed by withdrawal silenced him for good by September 1962. Photograph J.L. Stevenson, courtesy Hamish Stevenson.

A mid-1950s photograph of an immaculate, and probably ex-works 45534 E. TOOTAL BROADHURST of Edge Hill, on the turntable at Shrewsbury shed. Summer 1954 is my best guess – Ivatt top feed, hand rail yet to reach smoke deflector, no TV aerials apparent on nearby houses!

45534, fully modernised except for the speedometer yet to be fitted on the left-hand side, and electric warning flashes, at rest after bringing the 9.10am from Llandudno into Euston on 5 March 1960. This was our famed '10 to 2' train which, if it was on time, would enable us to regain our desks on time at junior school near to Northampton shed. Eventually the '11 plus' would elevate most of us to better (?) things at a train-less school on the other side of town. Those that failed the exam seemed at the time to have got a better deal, merely moving a few hundred yards nearer the action for another four years! Photograph Alec Swain, www.transporttreasury.co.uk

I would imagine that a Crewe North engine at Bridge of Dun was not far from the equivalent of a Kingmoor engine at the Euston end of the line. Having never had the benefit of a trawl through the 'shed book' of a Scottish spotter, I can only imagine. The photographer of 45535 SIR HERBERT WALKER K.C.B., may have been travelling on the 7.15am Glasgow Buchanan Street to Aberdeen express on 12 July 1952, as, in addition to this photograph at Bridge of Dun, he did the same at Forfar. Photograph J.L. Stevenson, courtesy Hamish Stevenson.

The crew of 45535 seem happy enough as it makes steady progress up towards Shap summit with an express on 8 July 1953. After the Aberdeen escapade above, 45535 went on loan to Edge Hill. On return to Crewe, the replacement 5A shedplate seen in this photograph looks to be a lopsided version of what might have been a 15A or a 25A plate. I have often wondered who was responsible for removing/refitting shedplates on transfers – it seems straightforward that the donor would start the ball rolling, but how do we account for reports stating that 'number so-and-so was seen at its new shed still bearing its original shedplate'. On a slightly different tack, New England Austerity 90549 was seen on Northampton shed carrying a 35A plate 18 months after the code, but not the allocation, was changed to 34E.

Compare the absence of a down sweep of the footplate under the cab of 45535 with that of the rebuilt Scot just visible on the left. Both are well coaled and ready for action in the yard at Camden loco on 17 April 1962. A look in the parent 'Book Of' on page 75 shows 45535 ex-Crewe works with the same patterns of dirt, even from the smoke deflector handholds. The green paintwork looks to have become rather more grubby within nine days than we might have appreciated. The loco had received a 'part paint' only, confined largely to the front end. Photograph Peter Groom.

Nameplate of 45535 obviously taken during its newly rebuilt British Railways black livery days. Despite a few visits to Crewe works over the years I never recollect seeing anyone painting lining onto engines, and being in a position in later years to see the same done on road vehicles, I think it a marvellous skill. Photograph J.L. Stevenson, courtesy Hamish Stevenson.

A decently red 5537 PRIVATE E. SYKES V.C., a Preston engine, at Barrow-in-Furness on 13 August 1939. Someone with time to spare had actually noticed that the comma (correctly) present on (4)5536 was missing in the case of 45537. First prize for engine picking goes to..... 'the unknown spotter'. Photograph R.J. Buckley, Initial Photographics.

Left. I doubt that an Edge Hill Patriot was a regular visitor to Watford shed, but a clean and tidy 45538 GIGGLESWICK, with local passenger headlamp, which may indicate an earlier failure, was there on an unrecorded date in July 1953. The Ivatt 2-6-2 tank would have been 41220. A later arrival at the shed was 41224, which became what we now call a celebrity, due to its retention of the BRITISH RAILWAYS in full on the tank side *into the early 1960s.* Photograph J. Robertson, www.transporttreasury.co.uk

Bottom left. Willesden had the use of 45539 E. C. TRENCH during the summer of 1959. The daubed 1A in place of a shedplate was something we were going to have to get more used to in the few years following. It is seen here at Shrewsbury at that time. The AWS gear had arrived earlier the same year.

Below. On 5 September 1959 Longsight's 45540 SIR ROBERT TURNBULL is approaching Shilton, between Nuneaton and Rugby with an up express which can almost be assumed to be from Manchester! I could not count the number of times that I had seen '55-40' on Manchester jobs over the years, but its eventual transfer away from Longsight seemed to presage bad times ahead – the more so because it was sent initially to Bushbury where the pending reduction in the London-Birmingham-Wolverhampton service was to do nothing for the wonderful Bushbury fleet of Jubilees. Photograph Peter Groom.

On its eventual arrival on the Midland division at Trafford Park, 45540 SIR ROBERT TURNBULL was back to differently routed Manchester-London expresses for a few months before continuing its downward spiral. Here he waits for time at Cheadle Heath with an up service on 8 June 1961. Nine days later he was off to Saltley – things were going from bad to worse! Photograph D. Forsyth, Paul Chancellor Collection.

Less than a month into its Midland journey, SIR ROBERT TURNBULL is passing Tyseley station with an up partially fitted freight, a Saltley working of some years standing. 45540, which was to survive only until early April 1963, was unique amongst the rebuilt Patriots in never receiving any version of the second tender emblem. That flapping tarpaulin on the fourth wagon would not be allowed today! Photograph Michael Mensing.

A filthy 45541 DUKE OF SUTHERLAND, devoid of a tail light, reversing out of Euston with the stock of what would have been an outer suburban semi-fast on Friday 5 August 1960. The LONDON-LIVERPOOL carriage board, as well as the spotters, possibly 'up from the country' and seemingly undisturbed by Authority, add even more nostalgia to the scene. Photograph Hamish Stevenson.

45542 had just been renumbered and suffered the painting out of LMS on the tender when photographed at Crewe works on 19 June 1949. A later picture in the parent 'Book Of' (page 83) indicates that it may have spent a period in unlined black with no indication of ownership. 45542 may possibly have later received BR mixed traffic black livery, but was in green by August 1953. This was of course the first of the 'officially new' Patriots. Photograph R.J. Buckley, Initial Photographics.

45542 has its work cut out coping with twelve coaches of an up express near Brock on 21 August 1953. Photograph A.W. Battson, www.transporttreasury.co.uk

It was a surprise to me to discover that sometime after transfer to Carnforth (24L) on or about 2 June 1962, 45543 HOME GUARD had managed to make it to Euston. Here are two end-on pictures of a well coaled 45543 taking water and manoeuvring round the yard at Camden shed, indicating that the return working was train 1L43.

45543 and 45550 were the last survivors of the original Patriots. They were stored in the burnt out remains of Preston shed until at least 20 July 1963. They were scrapped by September 1963, and the surprise in this photograph is that whilst the 24L shedplate has been removed from 45543, the nameplate is still attached. Photograph R. Butterfield, Initial Photographics.

45545 PLANET at St Rollox in October 1960, the elevated diesel shunter at a jaunty angle behind serving as the coal stage pilot. The name had only been bestowed on rebuilding and renumbering in November 1948.

Had I taken this photograph, I would have been trespassing, but Alec Swain had the privileged access of the senior railway officer; 45546 FLEETWOOD departs from Bletchley with a down relief on 28 March 1959. Photograph Alec Swain, www.transporttreasury.co.uk

I have previously bemoaned the fate of 45547 after it had been generally overhauled in April 1961, then being put to store in November 1961, never to work again. This photograph shows it in all its glory at Stafford shed in what can surely only be the immediate aftermath of the April 1961 repaint.

A daytime Birmingham-Edinburgh express climbs Shap unaided behind a bloodied (well, filthy) but unbowed 45548 LYTHAM ST ANNES on 19 July 1957. Photograph Les Elsey.

The approach of this doubleheader meant that any underlining in the ABC would be unlikely, discounting the possibility that the train engine might *just* be a Polmadie or Leeds Holbeck Scot! There were plenty of lads about who claimed to be able to tell if a rebuilt Scot or a rebuilt Patriot was approaching though in truth most of them probably relied on probability – the 71 versus 18 principle! I admit to taking the view that whatever ex-LMS 7P was on its way, it would soon be near enough for the numberplate to end the discussion. The combination of original 45550 piloting rebuilt 45521 RHYL (both of Edge Hill) is probably an instance of a train engine being piloted by one with no return working. The train is a Euston-Liverpool express about to enter Shugborough tunnel on Sunday 14 September 1958. Photograph Michael Mensing.

For thirteen years until January 1956 45550 was saddled with a high flat sided Stanier tender which (only my opinion) did nothing to enhance the balanced lines of a Patriot. Here the Carlisle Upperby engine is on Springs Branch shed on 4 April 1953 in the company of two locals; an ex-LNER J11 and an ex-LNWR D. Photograph A.G. Ellis, www.transporttreasury.co.uk

The last of the class to arrive before the Stanier Jubilees came, with the (initially unfulfilled) remit to relegate the Patriots to the second division. 45551 (12A) stands on home ground at Upperby on 5 June 1952. In the parent 'Book Of' (page 52) it is stated that 'All Patriots were used turn and turn about with engines in comparable power classes'. I have no difficulty with the 7P comparison, but I would have thought that, at least from the early 1950s until the bitter end (page 40) 'The better class of freight was becoming the best' for the parallel boiler engines. Photograph J.L. Stevenson, courtesy Hamish Stevenson.